Lorenabelle's Co-Dependent for Sure C~~~~~

Oatmeal, pecans, and chocolate chips create a cookie that Lorenabelle's therapy group now uses as a substitute for controlled substances. These chewy delights are best dunked in milk—at midnight.

Angst-Buster Risotto

This cheesy, soothing dish has a dramatic, mysterious, Fellini-movie quality, even though no one in his movies ever eats.

Apricot White Bread Hormone Replacement Therapy

A favorite of the Portland Ladies Needlepoint and Gun Club, these roll-up pastries are melt-in-the-mouth good and use that childhood staple, white bread, for a gooey, rich treat that forbids even one thought about cellulite.

COOKING FOR YOUR EVIL TWIN

ANN WALL FRANK, the staff food writer for the Portland *Oregonian*, is descended from a long line of Basque food lovers. Her culinary experience ranges from inventing hundreds of new ways to eat Wonder Bread to figuring out how to make Beef Wellington in a Betty Crocker E-Z Bake Oven. She believes that all food is "comfort food."

Ann Wall Frank

COOKING FOR YOUR EVIL TWIN

Devilishly Tempting Recipes for the Modern Woman

A PLUME BOOK

PLUME

Published by the Penguin Group
Penguin Books USA Inc., 375 Hudson Street, New York, New York 10014, U.S.A.
Penguin Books Ltd, 27 Wrights Lane, London W8 5TZ, England
Penguin Books Australia Ltd, Ringwood, Victoria, Australia
Penguin Books Canada Ltd, 10 Alcorn Avenue, Toronto, Ontario, Canada M4V 3B2
Penguin Books (N.Z.) Ltd, 182–190 Wairau Road, Auckland 10, New Zealand

Penguin Books Ltd, Registered Offices:
Harmondsworth, Middlesex, England

First published by Plume,
an imprint of Dutton Signet,
a division of Penguin Books USA Inc.

First Printing, April, 1994
1 3 5 7 9 10 8 6 4 2

℗ REGISTERED TRADEMARK—MARCA REGISTRADA

LIBRARY OF CONGRESS CATALOGING-IN-PUBLICATION DATA
Frank, Ann Wall.
Cooking for your evil twin : devilishly tempting recipes for the
modern woman / Ann Wall Frank.
p.   cm.
Includes index.
ISBN 0-452-27142-8
1. Cookery.   2. Cookery—Humor.   I. Title.
TX714.F72   1994
641.5—dc20   93-33382
                                                                            CIP

Printed in the United States of America
Set in Century Expanded and Kabel

Designed by Steven N. Stathakis

BOOKS ARE AVAILABLE AT QUANTITY DISCOUNTS WHEN USED TO PROMOTE PRODUCTS OR
SERVICES. FOR INFORMATION PLEASE WRITE TO PREMIUM MARKETING DIVISION, PENGUIN
BOOKS USA INC., 375 HUDSON STREET, NEW YORK, NEW YORK 10014.

Contents

✸

Bonding with Your Evil Twin: A Zero-Step Program

Somewhere inside you lurks an Evil Twin. Spot a chocolate torte on a bad day and she calls you like a siren. If you do not have a Twin—if you're always cheery, fair, forgiving, and you unwind with celery—put this book down, rush out and buy a copy of *Women Who Suppress Too Much*, and live happily ever after stuffing cloves in an orange.

Denial is a demon. If you solve your crises with a carrot stick, watch out. Your Twin is hunkered down deep in your subconscious stockpiling fudge for the revolution. Flesh her out. She is armed and dangerous.

The Evil Twin lives in the most primitive part of your brain, the limbic region. If she lived in a more recently formed cerebral locale, you would never wear a sharkskin bustier to your nephew's christening. You do not summon the Twin, she summons you. She is an intrepid dominatrix, filled with lusty appetites for food, lovers, and insults. The more cleverly disguised the Twin, the more handily she levels her blows. When you meet a woman who is wearing anklets, corduroy walking shorts, a turtleneck with whales (or ducks) on the collar, and a hair bow, and rose petals line her path and small forest animals gather in her wake, you are staring at a potential serial murderer or at least a man stealer. Just be aware of this.

Often, when therapists and other Twin-snuffers mention the Inner Child, it is really the Twin they mean, but their images are skewed. They refer to a fragile and vulnerable little girl in a polka dot dress and patent leather shoes clutching a lollipop who lives inside you and must be purged of the vile and bile of life. In truth, this is the Twin and she is clutching a hand grenade.

This book was written so that you can feed your Twin and she, therefore, can keep the grenade's pin in. She, unlike the contemporary, svelte, health-conscious, bikini-waxed, and trendy body she lives in, does not like tofu, endive salad, watercress sandwiches, and clear broth lunches. She likes to mainline chocolate. Maybe if you gave her more of it, she wouldn't have to rattle around in your subconscious hatching plots to drug your ex-husband and lock him up with a lonely Clydesdale.

With enough proper attention, the Twin will focus her attention on more innocuous antics such as getting drunk at wedding receptions and belting out "Wild Thing."

Here are some things you should know about your Evil Twin. The Twin is omnipresent: She is everywhere, kvetching in your ear, running your pantyhose, dashing into packed restaurants in front of elderly in wheelchairs and walkers. She is the one who, after months of counseling, when you finally have a breakthrough about the bum you've been supporting and don't have the guts to dump, trashes your therapist: "What does she know? She still wears underpants with the days of the week on them. Don't forget the way he blows in your ear. Pay his rent one more month. What can it hurt?"

The Twin is eternal: Like the billions of eggs in your ovaries, spots on your cuticles, and a talent for mixing cashmere and silk, you were born with her. The Twin is in your DNA. As a child, it was she who lathered the dog with a cream depilatory and blamed it on your younger brother. As an adult, she is more coy. She cannot resist a subtle tweak, no matter how trivial the subject. It is the Twin, who years after the friendly divorce and despite a decent friendship with your ex, says to him of his new fiancée, "Why, I adore her. I wish I had the nerve to do country and western hair."

The Twin is psychic: Somehow, she always knows when you're determined to stick to that diet. Just when you reach for another stick of celery, presto! she's thoughtfully stocked your fridge with Dove Bars, Snickers, Brie, beer, and pizza which she bought at the supermarket earlier while you were in a light trance.

The Twin is generous. Isn't it just like her to start the office collection for a birthday gift for the woman who tried to seduce your date at the Christmas party last year?

. . . *And creative:* Who else would think to buy her a total makeover for $10.99 including an Eva Gabor wig?

THE POSSESSION

Ever since I was nine and was caught shoplifting a Barbie doll, I have turned to food for solace. My mother, a feminist, did not believe a doll who came with a shelf bra and Spring-o-Later shoes had any value in my social engineering. But I still wanted Barbie. I wanted to have her long yellow lycra hair, her plastic perfect looks, her iron grip on Ken. So I tried to lift one from the toy store. I got caught, was admonished by the clerk, and left for King Kone where I devoured a shimmering, chocolate Hot Tin Roof sundae with Spanish peanuts and real whipped cream. This is the first time I remember meeting my Evil Twin. Not only did she encourage me to have seconds on the sundae, she suggested I leave the little Barbie experience out of my next confession. We bonded quick. Since then, I've found there's almost no experience the two of us can't get through together as long as we have a decent fork.

In my teens, Barbie started to get on my nerves. I was bored by her stiff ball gowns, her convent-issue active wear, and her accessories, especially Ken. It wasn't until Barbie got a kitchen that I began to really bond with her again. As a swinging single, she stocked her pad with frozen vegetables, canned soups, thin crackers, and juice. Had I set up the kitchen for Mattel, Barbie would have been drowning in a sea of José Cuervo, cinnamon rolls, onion pie, cheese enchiladas, and triple fudge brownies. And Ken wouldn't have shown his face without a sack of maple bars.

Since I have grown up, I've known a few real-life Barbies, but my true soul sisters have been endearingly flawed. Together, we've been through almost everything, including being jilted for Barbie knock-offs.

One thing binds our solace, though, and that is food. We obsess about it, talk about it, create it, cook it, and ultimately use it as the final comfort. And why not? It's a small indulgence for the kinds of things we endure—from a run on Mr. Wrongs to red alert bank accounts to impossible bosses to hormones that kick in at the car mechanic's.

Food, with its sweet and savory flavors, cellular-level comfort, and glorious aromas is rooted in childhood memories of snugly blankets, warm bosoms, and unlimited television. Food is gustatory salve that lies in the collective unconscious of anyone who has ever suffered a bruised knee or a bruised ego. It's food —chocolate, scones, warm breads, cookies—we friends send to each other when the resumé has been returned for the fiftieth time. When the guy with the collapsible handshake gets our promotion. When the car breaks down the day after the warranty expires. When lovers dump us. When the dog dies. Food, we know, isn't always sustenance for the body. It's more like soul batter. We pour it in, let it set for a while, and soon, we've risen a little.

I've never shoplifted since I tried to lift Barbie, but if I do, it won't be a toy. I envision my twilight years shuffling through the supermarket, support hose slipping around my ankles, pillbox hat perched on my head, loading macadamia nut truffles, rice pudding, and chocolate bars into my patent leather pocketbook.

Cooking for Your Evil Twin was written so that you, too, can slink out from the closet and anesthetize yourself with a natural wonder drug. The chapters were written with women in mind— we go from infancy to old age with food as our staff. We measure hormonal milestones with cravings for chocolate or salsa or warm bread. When we are babies we want pudding. When we are old we want pudding.

The first chapter, on chocolate, was written as tribute to the rite-of-passage into womanhood. Being female, chocolate cravings are molecular-based; our very DNA seems imbued with a fudge double helix. Most of adolescence is spent dreaming about boys, horses, and chocolate, the latter often the most affordable and faithful.

Breakfast foods have always been so comforting that the second chapter had to happen. Warm, crunchy, sweet, and stuck in that sleepy miasma of morning, a good breakfast is an antidote to the blues any time of day. Most women I know have a love/hate relationship with the early hours. Sleep is a drug they hate to leave as much as a good lover, but all of us (except maybe Charo) have something to do. Rich, golden, hot French toast helps, but it can also be just the ticket at midnight.

Remember back BFF (before fiber frenzy) when tampons, horseradish, and bread didn't have to be at least 13 percent oat bran and you could eat a gooey white bread sandwich without checking into the hospital? There is something about doughy bread that recalls the free-wheeling innocence of childhood. Pure and soft, it is a marriage bed for sublime, if unorthodox, spreads and soaks—from chocolate and peanut butter, to butter and sugar, to ripe tomatoes and balsamic vinegar. For many women, white bread wards off PMS like garlic does a vampire. There's something about flour that isn't mucked up with enough fiber to weave a welcome mat that keeps those hormones in check. Chapter 3 celebrates the best hormone replacement therapy since Rhett carried Scarlett up those stairs.

When I was a little girl and stayed with my grandma Lily, every day at noon, she pitched the card table and dressed it with a white linen cloth for lunch. We had homemade soup and watched "The Tennessee Ernie Ford Show." To this day as I taste good soup, thick with vegetables or creamy, rich and herb-flavored, I sing "Sixteen Tons" to myself. It was my first exposure to television commercials. Until then, I didn't know you could be nearly suicidal or else Prom Queen, depending on the smoothness of your skin. Advertisements gave my grandma endless giggles. Since then, I've always regarded advertising with a jaundiced eye and a craving for soup. Soup is a sacred meal. Chapter 4 offers soup recipes that nourish, comfort, and soothe when your grandma can't be there.

Rich, subtle, warm, soothing, delicious, and sometimes loath to rise, bread can be a lot like love. Sweet, chewy, and quick, or thick and cheesy, laden with sautéed vegetables, bread comforts in as many forms as we have moods. I used to watch my older sister put her babies down for a nap, slice us each a piece of coffeecake, and turn on her favorite soap operas. Soon, all her friends who watched the soap would call on the phone. They would laugh about how a kid in a playpen on the last episode was now graduating high school—and how they wished they could work that little trick. My sister and I still solve our own melodramas over coffee and good bread. Chapter 5 includes some of our favorite and most therapeutic bread recipes.

Aren't there times when the words Lite or Fat Free or Vegetarian or Meat Substitute make you want to beat a cow to death with your cruelty-free shoe, roast it over your Bic lighter, and have your own private Kon Tiki party? I am convinced that beef Stroganoff and meat loaf and macaroni and cheese produced a more innocent society. So I wrote chapter 6 on savories, which I believe satisfy a part of the limbic brain that wants us to do the bop.

Sometimes, the hormones align with the biorhythms that aspect the planets that throw off the vibrations that trance channel the auric rays to such a degree that you find yourself fantasizing about a ménage à trois with Nancy Reagan, Al Gore, and you. You crave the smell of dirty feet. You call a friend to read something fascinating aloud from the encyclopedia. Inexplicable! Just like certain food cravings ("No, I don't want a peanut butter and jelly sandwich. I want a peanut butter, banana, and mayonnaise sandwich with pepperoni"). Chapter 7 was written in hopes that some of your own quirky cravings are encoded in the great collective unconscious of bizarre combinations. My bad buying decisions, for example, can be attenuated only by graham crackers with cream cheese and chocolate chips. Go figure.

So, while I can't expect these recipes to cover the range of your very personal cravings, I hope they are a decent start. Mostly I hope they give you comfort. When your day is so rotten that the only images you can conjure are your thumb, a warm chocolate chip cookie, and your nightie, hop in your car, go home, and meet your Evil Twin. She'll show you how easy it is to use this book. Bon (Mega) Appetit!!!

Chapter One

The Twin, Adolescence, and Secondary Sex Characteristics, or Dumping Babs for the Big C

When the Twin reaches adolescence, her preoccupation with Barbie loosens, giving way to more sublime and mature obsessions. Chocolate, for one.

At about the same time that the ovaries ripen and begin dropping eggs down the fallopian tubes, breasts bud and idolatry of first ladies, fashion models, actresses, rock stars, and other girls' mothers begins, the hormone that wants you to have chocolate is released from the hypothalamus gland into the anterior pituitary, cheerleading the whole mystical tromp into womanhood.

The medical community's *Anatomical Cycle of Girls' Sexual Maturity and Chocolate Correlation Chart* is roughly as follows:

AGE	CHARACTERISTICS	CRAVING
Infancy–9	Hypothalamus concentrating on getting organs and limbs to line up.	ice cream, pudding
Prepubescent–Puberty	Hypothalamus and pituitary glands work in concert to create obsessive love of horses. Legs, teeth, hands are longer than most colts'. Crush on mother. Trade Barbie for M&M's.	M&M's
Puberty	Excessive crying, budding breasts, eyebrows grow together in one wing a la Frida Kahlo. Horses give way to boys. View *The Magic of Womanhood* film in Health Class. Desire for menstruation	candy bars

	takes parity with owning own male stallion named Blaze. Crush on father. Twin matures.	
Post-puberty– 20s–30s	Hypothalamus secretes cashmere hormone. Male Pattern Blindness occurs, disguising toads as good guys.	brownies
30s–40s	Hypothalamus begins releasing the "I'm finally getting it" hormone. Ambition, sex drive peaks, appearance of hair bumps.	tortes, fudge
50s–70s	Hypothalamus secretes the "I want to sell real estate" hormone. Barry Manilow fantasies, love of babies and puppies, trace signs of self-love begin.	berry pie

70s-   Replace Giorgio per-   ice cream, pudding
fume with camphor.
Love of poodles, ba-
bies, lavender, golf,
grandchildren, cookie
baking, other women,
and yourself. Craving
for bus tours. An-
swers to Life.

What the chart does not note is chocolate's manic entrance. One day, the prepubescent one is playing dolls and dreaming about offing Nancy Drew and taking over, the next she is stealing money from her mother's purse to buy a case of M&M's. Like smoking, the intake of chocolate is often done on the sly, in a closet, bathroom, or garage with a trusted friend. It's so good, it must be bad!

Chocolate milkshakes, sundaes, fudge brownies, candy bars, ice cream, pie—it's like a secret nation of allies. When no one understands you, chocolate is there—the creamy muse of self-love.

But to make the teen years even harder, chocolate has gotten a bad rap, blamed for everything from acne to mood swings.

The Twin, an intrepid researcher, wishes to slice through the bad press and suggest that the pain and anguish of puberty has nothing to do with the Big C. She further suggests the researchers do a few studies involving acne, mood swings, self-loathing, and sibling murder plots. The Twin suspects chocolate is an innocent scapegoat. Try examining free-floating insecurity, driver's license panic, nosy parents, space-crowding siblings, math anxiety, and Mr. Potato Head features, she advises. It will get better.

As you mature with chocolate, you will solve great problems and reach brilliant epiphanies during group eat-alongs. Chocolate will become a staple in your kitchen. Often, you will have it instead of dinner. You will dream about it.

Understand that unlike your love for Barbie, your love, even worship, of chocolate is here to stay. As an adult, often accompanying the onset of leg shaving or bouncing your first check, the Twin will introduce more sophisticated ways to enjoy its pleasures—in coffee and fine liqueurs for example. Or even better, in the bathtub.

There is only one thing to do with this milky, creamy, darkly delicious sweet treat. Surrender, draw a bath, and drown in its pleasures. Safe sin awaits with *chocolate*.

Kate's Howling at the Moon

Chocolate Peanut Bars

The only other thing that makes Kate howl is Patrick Swayze.

1 6-ounce package semisweet chocolate chips
1 6-ounce package vanilla chips
1 cup peanuts
1 cup peanut butter
½ cup (1 stick) butter or margarine

¼ cup evaporated milk
2 ounces butterscotch or vanilla pudding mix (not instant)
3¾ cups confectioners' sugar
½ teaspoon pure vanilla extract

Grease a small (10 × 6 or 10 × 8-inch) jelly-roll pan. In a large saucepan, melt the chips over low heat. Remove from the heat and stir in half of the peanuts and the peanut butter. Spread half of the mixture in the pan and chill in the fridge. Stir the remaining peanuts into the rest of the melted chip mixture, mix, and set aside.

In a large pan over low heat, melt the butter or margarine. Add the milk and stir in the pudding mix. Cook, stirring constantly, until slightly thickened. Don't boil. Remove from the heat, and stir in the sugar and vanilla. Cool slightly. Spread over the chilled mixture, cover the pan tightly, and chill in the fridge for 30 minutes. Cover with the remaining chocolate mixture. Cover and chill for another 30 minutes. Cut into squares.

Yield: 24 bars

He Drove Me to It

White Chocolate Chip Cookies

Cookies so good, you'll sit around and hope for PMS to hit.

1 cup (2 sticks) butter
1 cup granulated sugar
1 cup firmly packed brown sugar
1 egg
1 teaspoon pure vanilla extract
1 cup salad oil
1 cup rolled oats

½ cup shredded coconut
1 cup chopped hazelnuts
1 cup white chocolate or vanilla chips
3½ cups sifted all-purpose flour
1 teaspoon baking soda
1 teaspoon salt

Preheat the oven to 325° F.

In a large bowl cream together the butter and sugars. Add the egg, vanilla, and oil and mix well. Add the oats, coconut, nuts, and white chocolate chips, stirring well. Combine the flour, soda, and salt and add to the batter. Mix well and form into 1½-inch balls. Place them on an ungreased baking sheet and flatten with a fork dipped in ice water. Bake for 12 minutes.

Yield: 12 to 18 cookies

Lorenabelle's Co-Dependent

for Sure Chocolate Chippers

Lorenabelle's therapy group now uses these as a nice substitute for controlled substances. An excellent replacement for group therapy, these chewy delights are best eaten warm and dunked in milk.

1 cup (2 sticks) butter
1 cup granulated sugar
1 cup firmly packed light
   brown sugar
1 teaspoon pure vanilla extract
2 eggs
2 cups all-purpose flour

2½ cups rolled oats
1 teaspoon baking soda
1 teaspoon baking powder
1 16-ounce package semi-
   sweet chocolate chips
1½ cups chopped pecans

Preheat the oven to 350° F.

In a large bowl, cream the butter and sugars, then add the vanilla and eggs. Combine the flour, oatmeal, baking powder, and soda in a separate bowl. Mix the dry ingredients into the egg mixture. Stir in the chocolate chips and nuts and form the dough into 1-inch balls. Place them on a greased cookie sheet and bake for 12 to 14 minutes.

Yield: 18 to 25 cookies

Women Who Dine with

the Wolves Frosted Brownies

Ahhh, brownies. The official food of the Bad Hair Day Coalition.

1 cup (2 sticks) butter
3 tablespoons cocoa powder
1½ cups all-purpose flour
2 cups granulated sugar

4 eggs
1 teaspoon pure vanilla extract
1 cup chopped pecans

FROSTING
¼ cup (½ stick) butter,
   softened
1 teaspoon pure vanilla extract
4 cups confectioners' sugar

⅓ cup cocoa powder
½ cup evaporated milk

Preheat the oven to 350° F. Grease a 13 × 9 × 2-inch baking pan.

For the brownies, melt the butter with the cocoa in a medium saucepan and let cool. In a large bowl, combine the flour and sugar, then add the cocoa mixture. Start beating the mixture and add the eggs, one at a time, blending after each egg until dough is smooth. Fold in the vanilla and nuts.

Bake for 35 minutes. While the brownies are baking, make the frosting.

Cream the butter and vanilla and set aside. Combine the sugar and cocoa powder, then gradually blend it into the butter mixture, using an electric beater, alternating with the milk. Continue beating until the frosting is fluffy, about 4 minutes.

When the brownies have cooled completely, spread on the frosting. Cut into 18 pieces.

Yield: 18 brownies

Thigh Empowering Hot Cocoa

Cocoa knocks the Twin off her high horse and sweetens her. If only for a cup.

2 tablespoons dry cocoa mix
1 tablespoon confectioners' sugar
1 tablespoon powdered creamer

1½ cups whole milk
1 cup José Cuervo tequila—*just kidding*
Mini marshmallows or pink and white frosted animal cookies

Mix the dry ingredients together in the bottom of a large mug. Heat the milk until heated through and add to the mix. Add marshmallows or animal cookies.

Yield: 1 mugful

Choco-Peanut Quickie Tarts

These are what empowered James Brown to scream, "I feel good!"

1 15-ounce roll refrigerated
  peanut butter cookie dough
1 15-ounce roll refrigerated
  chocolate cookie dough

1 1-pound bag of miniature
  milk chocolate peanut butter
  cups
30 espresso beans

Preheat the oven to 350° F.

Let both cookie rolls stand at room temperature so that you can mix the two together with your hands. Chill 30 candy cups so you can take the paper off with your fingers instead of sucking it off in your mouth.

Grease miniature muffin pans. Scoop some dough into your hands, shape into a 1½-inch ball, and press into a greased muffin cup. Repeat for all the cups. Bake in the preheated oven for 8 to 10 minutes. Don't overbake. Remove from the oven and immediately put a candy cup (paper removed) and an espresso bean into each cookie-filled muffin cup. The heat of the dough will melt the chocolate perfectly. Let the pan cool to lukewarm. Refrigerate tarts for at least an hour unless you're desperate, in which case 10 minutes in the freezer will do. Gently lift each tart from the pan using the tip of a sharp knife.

Yield: 30 tarts

Ninja Denial Mud Pie

An easy recipe channeled to me by Chocta, a five-thousand-year-old CPA from Atlantis.

1 15-ounce roll refrigerated
  chocolate chip cookie dough
1 cup Häagen-Dazs coffee
  toffee ice cream, softened*
1 cup peanut butter fudge ice
  cream, softened

1 cup heavy cream
1 tablespoon sugar
½ teaspoon pure vanilla extract
2 1-ounce squares semisweet
  chocolate, grated

Preheat the oven to 350° F.

Press the cookie dough into a 10-inch buttered pie pan to form a pie shell. Bake for 10 minutes. Cool, then freeze for 15 minutes.

Spread the partially softened ice creams evenly over the pie crust. Freeze the pie for 15 minutes, or until the ice cream is firm.

Whip together the cream, sugar, and vanilla. Spread on the pie and add chocolate shavings just before serving.

Yield: 6 servings, but nobody says you have to get literal about it.

* You can also use mocha or jamoca almond fudge ice cream.

Midge's Metaphysical

Chocolate Caramels

On the twelfth caramel, Midge found truth. Hence the name.

2 cups sugar
1 cup half-and-half
4 1-ounce squares
  unsweetened chocolate

1 cup dark Karo syrup
1 cup (2 sticks) unsalted butter

Cook all the ingredients over medium-low heat, stirring constantly, until a small piece forms a hard ball when dropped into water. Pour into a greased pie plate and refrigerate for at least 2 hours. Cut into small pieces.

Yield: Approximately 24 caramels

Not Ready for Twelve Step

Anything Steamed Chocolate Pudding

Good steamed chocolate pudding is worth tunneling through a bunker for. This will keep the Twin at bay for days.

PUDDING
- 3 1-ounce squares semisweet baking chocolate
- 1 egg
- ¾ cup granulated sugar
- ½ cup half-and-half
- 2 tablespoons butter, melted
- 1 cup all-purpose flour
- 1 tablespoon baking powder
- 1 teaspoon pure vanilla extract
- ¼ teaspoon salt

HARD SAUCE
- 3 tablespoons butter
- ¼ cup chocolate syrup
- ⅔ cup confectioners' sugar
- ½ teaspoon pure vanilla extract
- Pinch salt

For the pudding, melt the chocolate in a double boiler over simmering water. In a bowl, beat the egg and sugar, then add all other ingredients including the melted chocolate. Turn into a buttered 1-quart mold and steam for 30 minutes. (To steam, place a rack in a large saucepan and pour boiling water up to the rack level. Place the mold with the pudding on the rack, cover the saucepan, and keep the water boiling over low heat.)

To unmold, run a knife around the edge of the mold, put a plate over the mold, and invert it.

For the hard sauce, cream the butter and syrup. Add and blend the remaining ingredients. Serve over the warm pudding.

Yield: 4 servings

Damage Control Chocolate

Crumb Pudding

Twin serving suggestion: Yourself.
Wondering what to do with that leftover cake? As if . . .

2 cups any kind of cake crumbs
  (devil's food is wonderful)
1 pint half-and-half
1 ounce sweet chocolate (see
  Note)
2 egg yolks

Pinch salt
½ teaspoon pure vanilla extract
2 bananas, sliced (optional)
2 tablespoons sugar
Whipped cream (optional)

Preheat the oven to 375° F.

In a double boiler, cook the cake crumbs, half-and-half, and chocolate, stirring often. When the mixture is gooey, remove from the heat and add the egg yolks, salt, and vanilla. Turn into a buttered, 8-inch square baking dish and bake for 10 minutes. Mix the banana slices, if using, with the sugar and place on the pudding, or sprinkle just the sugar over the top. Brown under the broiler for about 2 minutes. Top with whipped cream, if desired. Serve warm.

Yield: 2 servings

Note: Baker's German's sweet chocolate bar is best.

Won't Bite Back Chocolate Chews

Worth losing some cheap dental work for.

20 graham crackers, crushed
1 cup sweetened condensed
  milk
1¼ cups semisweet chocolate
  chips

½ cup chopped pecans
¼ teaspoon pure vanilla extract

Preheat the oven to 350° F.

Combine all the ingredients and spread the mixture into a greased 8-inch square pan lined with wax paper. Bake for 30 minutes. Cut while still warm.

Yield: 12 to 16 squares

Who Invented Swimsuits Anyway?

Gooey Fudge Macadamia Nut Cake

A gift from King Kahuna to his mail-order bride.

CAKE
1 cup (2 sticks) butter, room
   temperature
2 cups granulated sugar
3 eggs, lightly beaten
1 cup chocolate syrup

1½ cups cake flour
1 cup coarsely chopped
   macadamia nuts
1 teaspoon pure vanilla extract

ICING
2 tablespoons butter, melted
2 cups confectioners' sugar
3 tablespoons Cafe Mocha or
   other flavored instant coffee
   powder

1 teaspoon pure vanilla extract
¼ cup heavy cream

Preheat the oven to 375° F.

   For the cake, cream the butter and sugar in a large bowl.
Add the eggs and chocolate syrup alternating with the flour. Add

the nuts and vanilla. Bake in a shallow, greased 12 × 8-inch pan for 35 to 40 minutes, or until a knife inserted in the center comes out clean.

Mix all the icing ingredients together while the cake is baking and spread over the cake as soon as you remove it from the oven. If the icing is too stiff, add a little hot water.

Yield: 8 servings

Note: This cake is dense and chewy—almost gooey.

Kate's Kiss Off

Chocolate Peanut Pie

Donna Reed, eat your heart out.

24 chocolate wafer cookies

FILLING

8 ounces softened cream
   cheese
1 cup sugar
1 cup creamy peanut butter

2 tablespoons butter, melted
1 cup heavy cream
1 tablespoon pure vanilla
   extract

TOPPING

4 ounces semisweet chocolate
2 tablespoons butter
2 tablespoons salad oil

1/8 teaspoon pure vanilla extract
Crushed peanuts, white and
   dark chocolate shavings
   (optional)

For the crust, crush the wafers and pat the crumbs into a greased 9-inch pie pan, pressing evenly onto the bottom and sides.

    For the filling, whip the cream cheese until fluffy. Slowly mix in the sugar, peanut butter, and melted butter. Whip the cream and vanilla until firm. Blend ⅓ cup of the whipped cream into the peanut butter mixture. Fold this mixture into the remaining whipped cream until totally blended. Fill the pie shell, smooth the top, and chill in the freezer for at least 20 minutes.

For the topping, combine all but the optional ingredients and melt them in the top of a double boiler until the chocolate melts. Cool slightly. Spread the mixture on the cooled peanut butter pie starting from the center and working out. Chill or freeze until ready to serve.

If desired, decorate the top with crushed peanuts and white and dark chocolate shavings before serving.

Yield: 6 to 8 servings

Chapter 2

The Twin's Private Breakfast Club

Nothing takes the spin off a morning faster than a diet. Who wants to bolt from bed in the morning, leap onto the stationary bike, and then stare down one ounce of rice puffs with a half cup of skim milk and bonus strawberry? Or maybe you even fast. "What next, stigmata?" cries the Twin, when you greet the day with such martyrdom.

The Twin is not a morning entity. She often chooses this time to recharge, sucking, like Dracula, the soul of her victims. Liquid breakfasts fuel her depravity.

Even if you generally greet the morning like Julie Andrews

in *The Sound of Music*, there are days when you feel more like Quasimodo, hump and all.

Aside from waking up with someone you inexplicably want to ax murder, other clues to the Twin's Private Breakfast Club Appearance are bent hair that won't straighten, pantyhose that runs when removed from the package with a crotch that begins at your knees, and makeup that will not go on despite a good trowel.

Why do mornings drag such old stuff from the margins of our minds? Why are mornings sometimes so melancholy? And if they are—if that rain is beating against that loose window pane and the sun's rays are made weak and thin by a gray shadow cast over your bed, why couldn't you look like Simone de Beauvoir or Greta Garbo—angst-ridden but beautifully tragic, instead of just in need of a serious brow tweezing and some floss? Why do we wake up thinking about food?

Men can solve crises over sausage, eggs, French toast with syrup and butter, hash brown potatoes, fresh squeezed orange juice, and coffee with cream. "Good point," they'll say, shoving two eggs and a sausage link into their mouths. "Let's go with the lumber straddle and use it to leverage Bolivia." They can actually devour this meal and continue their day, without rewinding a tape of the menu. Men have also never given a thought to combination skin.

Women will count the calories using every method from the metric system to an abacus to see if they can be computed lower.

If morning doesn't become you, you've probably been acting too much like Melanie in *Gone With The Wind*. You went to bed happy. During the night, the Twin, bored with your program, is miffed. You ignored her early warning signals when you made a pot of coffee without the grounds and hit your shin against the exercise bike. The cereal and skim milk was the last straw.

Quietly, she instructs you to skip washing your hair, apply lots of green eye shadow, dig out that old pep club sweater and pull it on over leggings, pick a fight with anybody, and start smoking again.

This done, you notice it's almost time to leave for work. There are only seconds left to examine your life and conclude its vast emptiness and lack of accomplishment. All of a sudden you're at your desk reaching for the valium and a revolver, and you're writing out your will. Then you remember your mother would have you buried in an outfit from L. L. Bean.

There's only one antidote to the Twin's antics at this point. Slip into your warm robe and fuzzy slippers, make some cocoa, and ask her to stay for warm, nourishing, soothing, inner-child-hugging breakfast.

Pannekoeken

(Translation: Fattenthighen)

This recipe was a gift from my German foreign exchange Twin Brunhilde. Seems comfort food is multilingual.

4 eggs
4 cups sifted cake flour
4 cups whole milk
1 teaspoon salt

Butter for frying
Maple syrup
Confectioners' sugar
Lemon wedges (optional)

Beat the eggs, then stir in the cake flour alternately with the milk. Add the salt.

Melt butter in a large heavy skillet and pour in just enough batter to cover the bottom. Brown for about 1 minute, then turn and brown the other side. Serve with syrup and/or confectioners' sugar and serve hot. Great with fresh lemon squeezed over the syrup.

Yield: 6 pannekoeken

Calorically Incorrect

Baked Frenchies

Is there anything better than warm French toast? This will replace therapy for a year.

2 tablespoons light or dark Karo syrup
½ cup (1 stick) butter
1 cup firmly packed brown sugar
12 to 14 slices extra thick French bread or challah bread

5 eggs
1 cup melted pralines and cream ice cream or maple nut ice cream
1 teaspoon pure vanilla extract
Pinch salt
Butter, syrup, or jam

Combine the corn syrup, butter, and brown sugar in a saucepan and simmer until syrupy. Pour the mixture into a 13 × 9-inch casserole dish. Place the bread over the mixture. In a bowl, beat together the eggs, ice cream, vanilla, and salt and pour over the bread. Cover the dish and let stand in the refrigerator overnight.

Preheat the oven to 350° F. Uncover the pan and bake for 45 minutes. Serve warm with butter, syrup, or jam—or all three.

Yield: 6 servings

Gorging Your Inner

Child Waffles

Serving suggestion: All United Nations Peace Treaty breakfasts.

½ cup (1 stick) margarine
2 tablespoons firmly packed
   light brown sugar
2 eggs, separated
1 ripe banana, mashed
1 cup plus 1 tablespoon cake
   flour
1 tablespoon baking powder

Pinch salt
¾ cup heavy cream
Maple syrup
1½ cup chopped toasted
   hazelnuts (see Note)
Butter
Strawberries

In a large bowl, cream together the margarine and sugar. Add the egg yolks and banana and blend. In another bowl, mix the flour, baking powder, and salt. Using low speed on the mixer, alternately add the heavy cream and flour mixture to the egg yolk mixture. Add 1 teaspoon of maple syrup. Beat the egg whites until stiff and fold into the batter. Spoon the batter onto a preheated waffle iron and sprinkle with 2 to 2½ tablespoons of hazelnuts per waffle.

Cook according to manufacturer's instructions, then slather on butter, syrup, and fresh strawberries.

Yield: Serves 10 of your inner children

Note: Oven-toast hazelnuts by placing them on a cookie sheet in a 350° F. oven for 8 to 10 minutes.

"I'm Telling Mom" Oatmeal

So what if it has the consistency of school glue. Oatmeal heals.

1⅓ cups cold water
Pinch salt
¾ cup regular rolled oats

Butter, brown sugar, honey,
jam, or cream

Mix water, salt, and oats in a small saucepan. Bring to boil over high heat. Lower the heat and boil gently, for 5 minutes.

Remove the pan from the heat and let sit for 3 minutes, covered. Stir in your choice of butter, brown sugar, honey, jam, or cream. Another nice touch is a raisin silhouette of Jane Fonda as you'd like to see her look, if you get my drift.

Yield: 1 serving

Frenzied French Toast

Another quicker and sinfully delicious French toast recipe.

1 egg
½ cup milk
Pinch salt
1 teaspoon sugar
1 tablespoon maple syrup

½ teaspoon pure vanilla extract
3 tablespoons butter
4 1-inch-thick slices of day(s) old egg bread, cinnamon bread, or challah bread

In a shallow bowl, beat the egg, milk, salt, sugar, syrup, and vanilla. In a heavy skillet, melt the butter over medium heat until it foams, but don't let it brown.

Soak both sides of the bread in the egg mixture and fry in the butter over medium heat, browning both sides. Serve hot with more butter and hot syrup.

Yield: 1 serving—barely

Thumb-Sucking Rice Pudding

Oral gratification at its baby-food finest.

1 egg, well beaten
¼ cup granulated sugar
2 tablespoons firmly packed
  brown sugar
1 cup half-and-half
1 cup cooked white rice
¼ cup raisins

1 small apple, peeled, cored,
  and diced
1 teaspoon pure vanilla extract
Dash nutmeg
Pinch salt
½ cup heavy cream

Preheat the oven to 350° F.

In a large bowl, combine all ingredients except the cream and stir until well blended. Pour into a buttered 1-quart baking dish. Bake the pudding in the middle of the oven for 20 minutes. Remove and stir, then return to the oven and bake for another 15 or 20 minutes, or until firm. Remove and stir in the heavy cream.

Cool to room temperature and serve, or chill and serve, but warm is more womb-like.

Yield: 6 servings

Mom's Tater Patties

Mooshy, gooshy, fragrant, and satisfying. Fun to eat and play with.

3 cups cold mashed potatoes
(instant is fine)
1 egg
¼ teaspoon salt
½ teaspoon cracked black
pepper

¼ teaspoon garlic powder
1 tablespoon dried rosemary
1 cup grated Cheddar cheese
Olive oil and butter for frying
Catsup (optional)

Mix together all the ingredients, except the oil and butter, and form into patties. Sauté over medium heat in butter and olive oil for 3 to 4 minutes each side or until well browned.

Great with catsup.

Yield: 2 servings

Shredded Wheat Boats

What Einstein was eating when he came upon the Theory of Relativity.

¼ cup sugar
1 tablespoon cinnamon
2 tablespoons softened butter

2 large shredded wheat biscuits
Milk or half-and-half

Preheat the oven to 350° F.

Mix together the sugar and cinnamon.

Spread one tablespoon of the butter on each biscuit and sprinkle each with half of the cinnamon-sugar mixture. Bake in a buttered pie plate for 5 minutes. Remove, place in a bowl, and add fresh milk or half-and-half.

Yield: 1 serving

Cosmic Corned Beef

Hash and Eggs

This dish has that pioneer-woman touch that goes so well with a gingham apron and stiletto heels.

3 tablespoons butter
1 small onion, chopped
¼ cup chopped green or red pepper
½ cup minced cooked corned beef
1 red potato, boiled, peeled, and diced

⅓ cup beef stock
½ cup frozen corn
½ teaspoon dried rosemary
2 eggs
Pinch salt
Freshly ground black pepper
Catsup

In a small, heavy skillet, melt the butter over medium heat and sauté the onion and green pepper for 5 minutes, or until soft. Add the corned beef, potato, stock, corn, and rosemary and stir until heated through.

With the back of a spoon, make a hollow in the center of the hash. Break the eggs into a cup and carefully slip the eggs into the hollow. Add salt and pepper to the eggs. Cover and cook over low heat for 10 minutes or until the eggs are set. Serve hot with catsup.

Yield: 2 servings

Chapter Three

Unnatural Acts with White Bread: PMS—Eating for the Siberian Army and Dressing for Secession

We are shopping at Nordstrom, but we should be shopping at Temporarily Insane-R-US. Kate, Lynn, and I all have *serious* PMS. The Evil Twin is guiding each of our fashion selections like Coco Chanel on acid.

"My face would fill the window of a 747, it's so swollen," Kate says, studying the mirror. "Better to look at your outfit," I say. "You sure you want that?"

"What's wrong with it?" She is testy. I understand. I myself am dressed in a $300 gypsy gown that I bought last month about this time. Lynn is still in the dressing room mainlining a Snickers bar.

"I just think in a week you'll hate red cowboy boots and leather jackets with thirty pounds of chains."

"I think you're wrong," Kate says. "You could dress a little more hip. Only Manuel Noriega wears that much khaki."

Mean. We get mean to each other, our blood coursing with Close Out Sale hormones and an appetite for luaus, the unspoken, immutable laws for loving friendship temporarily on ice. Each month we cruise department stores, thrift shops, and strangers' attics for clothes that sparkle and shine and shimmer and shake.

The Evil Twin has no taste. In five days your closet can look like the wardrobe from *Les Miserables*.

Day 1, PMS, we are Tinkerbell, Day 2, Ann Margret in *Viva Las Vegas*. We are fugitives of salt retention, drunk with credit-card power, women who dine with the wolves.

Then, a week later, systems all humming at ground zero, we're back in black.

It wasn't my mood that sent me to the gynecologist, it was my credit-card debt and a closet full of chiffon and metal.

I was the first to go for help. I tell Kate and Lynn about it over lunch.

ME: Dr. Silver says a lot of PMS is just fatigue. He said, "Ann, try to catch a nap every day, even if only for ten minutes." And I think he's—

LYNN: Why are you "Ann" and he is "Dr. Silver"? Like Jessie

on "General Hospital." Remember, for years she kowtowed to precious Dr. Hardy—even had an affair with him—I think even *married* him and still called him Dr. Hardy even after he dumped her—again and again . . .

KATE: Are you going to get fries?

LYNN: I'm just having the salad bar.

No wonder. She could feed the third world with the chili, potato salad, macaroni, fried chicken wings, cheese, and garlic bread that are nestled up to the lettuce, tomatoes, and cucumbers on her plate.

KATE: The salad bar? For God's sake! May I remind you that a sneeze guard does not a diet make?

ME: So anyway, he asks me to describe my symptoms and I tell him I am comparison shopping for automatic weapons and crying over Rod McKuen poems.

LYNN: Does he still wear those crepe-soled shoes?

KATE: I think he buys them at a tire store. I wonder if they still have those purple boots with the platform heels at Nordstrom.

ME: Don't get them. They make you look like an "I Dream of Jeannie" extra. Anyway, chocolate is out. So is caffeine, alcohol, salt, and sugar. Also, he said B vitamins wouldn't hurt . . .

LYNN: You ate my brownie.

KATE: Hormone Replacement Therapy.

LYNN: What about fringe?

KATE: Huh?

LYNN: There's a fringed cowhide jacket with a solid red rhinestone back at The Limited. Let's go.

ME: Dibs.

The Evil Twin, having picked up the scent of a swollen cache of non-durables, is leading us to a fresh kill. Later on, we stop at the store for the ritual PMS staple—white bread, for the makings of something gooey, gross, and forbidden. Plain and doughy, a square of innocence, free from the responsibilities of post-fiber America and its Surgeon General warnings. We are kids again, squishing it in balls and rolling it up like dollar bills, dipping it in peanut butter, jelly, and melted chocolate. Hormones be damned. Oh, what we can do with high hormones and the simplest of harvests!

Apricot Joy

This is a dish that Alice, the maid on "The Brady Bunch," might have cheerfully made, then scarfed down alone in the closet.

½ pound soft dried apricots (see Note)
2 cups cold water
¼ cup (½ stick) butter
2 English muffin halves, or 2 slices poppy seed or white bread, crusts removed and cubed

½ cup firmly packed brown sugar
¼ teaspoon cinnamon

Preheat the oven to 300° F.

Place the apricots in an uncovered saucepan, add the water, and bring to a boil. Simmer for 30 minutes. Let cool and drain, reserving the liquid.

Generously butter a deep 1-quart casserole. Place a layer of apricots on the bottom, add a layer of bread cubes, and sprinkle with brown sugar. Repeat the layers until the ingredients are used up. Add the cinnamon to the apricot liquid and pour over the "casserole." Bake covered for 30 to 35 minutes.

Yield: 6 servings

Note: You can also use dried peaches or apples.

45

Apricot White Bread Hormone

Replacement Therapy

A favorite of the Portland Ladies Needlepoint and Gun Club.

4 slices fresh, white "balloon"
   bread (see Note), crusts
   removed
2 teaspoons soft butter

¼ cup apricot fruit preserves
1 teaspoon cinnamon
¼ cup sugar

Preheat the oven to 325° F.

Roll each slice of the bread thin with a rolling pin. Spread each with approximately ½ teaspoon butter and 1 tablespoon preserves. Starting on the diagonal, roll each slice of bread into a tube. Mix cinnamon and sugar together. Sprinkle generously with cinnamon-sugar mixture and place on a greased cookie sheet with the seam down. Bake for 10 to 15 minutes or until brown. Serve warm.

Yield: 4 rollups

Note: "Balloon" bread is that white, squishy fiber-free bread that you usually only buy at Thanksgiving to make stuffing.

Eve's Apple Pie

Quick, easy, and juicy with a crisp crust. More than we can say for Adam.

4 slices white bread, crusts
   removed
Butter for buttering bread
1 Granny Smith apple, peeled,
   chopped, and divided in half

1 teaspoon cinnamon
¼ cup sugar

Preheat the oven to 375° F.

Roll bread slices thin with a rolling pin. Butter each slice on one side.

Mix the cinnamon and sugar together. Sprinkle about ½ teaspoon of the cinnamon sugar mixture and half of the chopped apple onto the buttered side of two slices of bread. Top each slice with another slice of bread, butter side down, and press the "crust" together with a fork. Sprinkle the tops with more of the cinnamon-sugar mix and bake for about 10 minutes, or until brown.

Yield: 2 pies

I Love My Blankey

Cinnamon Toast

Comforting to eat while watching Saturday morning cartoons, or The Terminator.

2 pieces of bread—cinnamon raisin or white—or 2 English muffin halves

Butter
¼ teaspoon cinnamon mixed with 1 tablespoon sugar

Toast the bread, then spread generously with butter and sprinkle with the cinnamon-sugar mix.

For extra crispiness, pop under the broiler for a few seconds.

Yield: 1 serving

Chocolate Bar Sandwich

A little peanut butter spread on the bread makes a nice variation of this clever sandwich so enjoyed by the Queen of England at her royal teas.

Butter
2 slices fresh white soft bread

1 6-ounce milk chocolate
   candy bar

Butter both slices of the bread on one side. Break the chocolate bar into squares and place on the buttered side of one slice, topping with the other slice, butter side down. In a small frying pan, melt 2 tablespoons of butter over low heat and grill the sandwich over medium-low heat for about 2½ minutes on each side.

Goes well with beer.

Yield: 1 sandwich

Desperately Seeking Sugar

Instant High Sandwich

Colorful cake-decorator beads may replace the sugar if it's your birthday.

1 tablespoon granulated or firmly packed brown sugar

1 tablespoon butter
2 slices white bread

Combine the sugar with the butter and make the first decent sandwich spread since process cheese came on the market.

Yield: 1 sandwich

Anna Freud's Crunchy Naner Dog

Nice to eat alone in a Freudian slip and rubber thongs.

1 slice white "balloon" bread
  (see Note)
2 tablespoons crunchy peanut
  butter

1 small, peeled banana
Jelly of choice

Spread the bread with the peanut butter and roll it around the banana like a hot dog. Dip in the jelly jar if desired.

Yield: 1 dog

Note: "Balloon" bread is that doughy white bread you can roll into a dense ball and sits in your stomach for about 3 days.

Miracle Thigh Open-Face

Cheese Sandwich

All calories escape from any sandwich served open faced.

1 teaspoon butter
2 slices any white bread
2 slices American or Cheddar
  cheese
Miracle Whip salad dressing

1 tablespoon chopped green
  onions (optional)
1 tablespoon sunflower seeds,
  shelled

Lightly butter the bread, add the cheese, and place under the broiler for about 45 seconds or until the cheese melts. Add a dollop of Miracle Whip, the chopped green onions, if using, and sunflower seeds and slide under the broiler for another 10 seconds.

Yield: 1 open-face sandwich

Toad in a Hole

I know. You thought there were enough toads in your life.

1 slice white bread
2 tablespoons butter

1 egg
Salt and pepper to taste

Cut a small circle out of the bread with the open end of a glass. Stuff the round center in your mouth.

Heat the butter in a small sauté pan over medium heat and drop in the bread, letting it brown about 1 minute.

Crack the egg perfectly in the center and cook until it is set. Remove with a spatula. Salt and pepper to taste.

Yield: 1 toad

Dysfunctional Tomatoes

Apologies for the balsamic vinegar. At least there's no pesto or sun-dried tomatoes in this book.

1 28-ounce can whole tomatoes with liquid
½ cup firmly packed dark brown sugar
¼ cup butter, melted
Pinch salt and pepper
1 teaspoon balsamic vinegar
⅓ cup any kind of dry white bread, cubed
⅓ cup bread crumbs

Drain the tomatoes. Add the sugar, butter, salt, pepper, vinegar, and dry bread and stir. Simmer very gently on the stove for 2½ hours, adding water if necessary. Put into a buttered 1-quart baking dish. Preheat the oven to 375° F. Sprinkle the tomato mixture with bread crumbs and bake uncovered for 30 minutes, or until browned.

Yield: 4 servings

Chapter Four

Thin Thighth in Thirty Dayth and Other Advertithing Lieth

If you're like me, your Evil Twin likes to wait until your self-loathing quotient is really high—say after you've rented *Body Heat* for the fortieth time to curse God for giving Kathleen Turner the body you were supposed to have because you would have been so much more charitable with it—to suggest that, together, you find some short cuts for weight loss and beauty enhancement.

Women's magazines are helpful. Even though you haven't bought a *Cosmopolitan* in twenty years, the Twin will say, "Oh what the hell, don't you even want to know how to make a bikini wax a sensual experience?" So you buy the *Cosmo*, and about fifteen other magazines that promise that if you're thin enough, blonde enough, charming enough, ambidextrous enough, smart (but not too smart) enough, and rich enough, you can finally dump what's his name and land a count. Or at least a straight man. Maybe even with a job.

Time to scan. Put on your favorite old bathrobe, a pair of warm socks, and a favorite record. Pour a glass of wine.

You will barely have turned the magazine page when the Twin starts harping. "There's one," she will say, pointing to an ad for face cream. Where? you ask. "Right there under 'Men Seeking Men.' What else do you know that will eliminate wrinkles while you a) stage a corporate takeover; b) polish furniture; or c) dine with unsuspecting friends at a posh restaurant."

I happen to know one of these potions is actually a scary glue that dries like a shrink wrap and freezes back the face like you're the hood ornament of a 747, I tell her. "So smile before you apply it," she snaps.

"How about this one?" says the Twin, stopping at the Miracle Pill that burns thigh fat like a furnace while we sleep. I'm not sure. It's hard to imagine waking up and saying, "*My God*, my thighs are completely skinny and long and hairless and perfect just like the jar of Thigh-B-Goddess said!"

I'm a skeptic, though staring at pictures of Michelle Pfeiffer is lowering my usual impeccable standards for demanding truth in advertising. The Twin and I scan on, noting that the most convincing ads are for products that are imported from Europe and include dirt from the holy lands or Uranus or that share a close relationship with the Dead Sea Scrolls. The befores (Phyllis Diller, pre-cosmetic surgery) and afters (Linda Evans, early "Big Valley"), do not at all amaze product inventor Hungarian plastic surgeon Dr. Mihkeaveal Dorvesskkilsvvoeha who attributes his formula to an interpretation of a secret passage in Upanishad writings.

Melinda's Twin recently talked her into that funny little chin strap that you hook behind your ears to kind of cradle your double chin in latex while you sleep. "I figure with the right makeup application, I can wear it all day," she says. "Though those ear straps are making me a little testy."

Melinda, who actually is in no need of this stuff, is an expert on mail-order beauty. "I draw the line on that woman who grinds up all the pearls and wants you to smear them all over your face," she says. "I don't even own a strand of pearls and she wants me to smear them over my upper lip? I don't think so."

Years ago, Lynn's Evil Twin talked her into Vacu-Pants and Slim Skins. They were obscene looking knee-length plastic shorts whose manufacturers claimed could suck off fat with a vacuum cleaner hose through a hole in the pants. She didn't lose weight, probably because she was using an upright, but she still has the pants for summer beach parties and Saran Wrap galas.

I say we start liking the whole body enchilada, take the money that could be spent on this junk, and buy fixin's for soup.

Chicken Soup in Recovery

This soup takes a little time, but it peels the skin off of what ails you.

STOCK:
1 small (2-to-3-pound) chicken
Olive oil
½ teaspoon rosemary
½ teaspoon oregano
½ teaspoon basil
½ teaspoon sea salt
6 cups water
3 celery ribs with tops
1 turnip, peeled and cut into small pieces
1 carrot, chopped
1 onion, unpeeled
1 clove
1 clove garlic, crushed
6 peppercorns
1 tablespoon chopped fresh parsley

SOUP:

1 cup water

1 teaspoon Kitchen Bouquet

2 carrots, peeled and cut into 1-inch pieces

2 ribs celery, cut into 1-inch pieces

1 small zucchini, chopped into ½-inch pieces

1 bay leaf

1 teaspoon salt

½ teaspoon black peppercorns

1 onion, chopped

¼ cup chopped fresh parsley

Preheat the oven to 400° F.

Rub the chicken with the olive oil, rosemary, oregano, basil, and sea salt. Place in a roaster pan and bake until the juices run clear, approximately 15 minutes per pound.

Remove the chicken from the pan. Pour 1 cup of water into the bottom of the roaster and place over medium heat and deglaze (scrape brown bits from bottom). Transfer to a large soup pot and add the remaining water. Skin and bone the chicken and add skin and bones to the stock pot, along with all the remaining stock ingredients. Bring to a boil, reduce heat, and simmer for 2½ to 3 hours. Cut the chicken into bite-size pieces. Strain the stock into a large saucepan, discarding the skin, bones, and pulp. Skim off any fat from the top of the stock.

Add all the soup ingredients and the chicken meat to the stock, bring to a boil, and simmer for another 30 to 40 minutes.

Yield: Serves 4 or 1 bad cold

Cheap Thrills Broccoli Bisque

True, the Twin is not normally a broccoli fan. But if George Bush hates it . . .

1 cup sliced leeks
1 cup sliced mushrooms
3 tablespoons butter
3 tablespoons flour
3 cups good chicken broth
1 cup creamed corn
1 cup broccoli florets,
   chopped fine

1 cup heavy cream
½ cup shredded smoked
   Gouda or Cheddar cheese
Salt
Cracked black pepper

Sauté the leeks and mushrooms in the butter in a saucepan until they are tender but not brown. Add the flour with a wire whisk and cook, stirring constantly until bubbling. Remove from the heat and gradually add the chicken broth. Return to the heat and cook, stirring constantly until it becomes thick and smooth. Add the corn and broccoli. Reduce the heat and simmer for about 20 minutes. Blend in the cream and cheese and simmer until the cheese melts. Salt and pepper to taste.

Yield: 6 to 8 servings

Patty's Buttermilk Soup

Patty believes buttermilk is a Twin anti-inflammatory.

5 strips lemon peel
1 tablespoon fresh lemon juice
4 egg yolks
½ cup sugar

1 quart buttermilk
4 thin lemon slices for garnish
Slivered almonds for garnish

Put the lemon peel, juice, egg yolks, and sugar in a food processor and process for 1 minute. Add the buttermilk and blend for about 10 seconds. Let stand overnight in the refrigerator. Serve very cold with a thin lemon slice and almonds as garnish.

Yield: 4 servings

Our Lady of Perpetual

Misery Corn Chowder

Is there something with nuns and corn or is it just the Twin's wicked imagination?

3 cups water
6 potatoes, peeled and diced
1 small onion, chopped
2 small or 1 large clove garlic, minced
½ cup chopped celery
½ teaspoon salt
½ teaspoon fresh ground pepper
⅛ teaspoon sage

¼ teaspoon thyme
½ bay leaf
4 cups whole-kernel corn (frozen is okay)
2 cups hot milk
4 strips bacon, cut into small pieces
¼ cup chopped green pepper
½ cup minced green onions
3 tablespoons chopped parsley

Bring the water to a boil in a soup pot. Add the potatoes, onion, garlic, and celery. Return the water to a boil and add the seasonings. Cover and simmer over medium heat for about 15 minutes, or until the potatoes are tender but not mushy. Add the corn. Add the milk and stir frequently for about 5 minutes so the chowder doesn't stick to the pan. In a skillet, sauté the bacon for 2 minutes, then add the green pepper and green onions and sauté briefly. Stir into the simmering chowder then add the parsley. Remove the bay leaf and add salt and pepper to taste.

Yield: 4 to 6 servings

The Beaning of Life Soup

The combination of sausage and syrup began as a facial mask for the Twin and evolved into this tasty soup.

1 pound Italian sausage links
sliced in pennies
1 cup chopped onion
1 cup sliced carrots
1 cup chopped celery with
tops
1 10- or 12-ounce can chicken
broth
1 tablespoon maple syrup
1 tablespoon Dijon mustard
2 8- or 10-ounce cans cooked
pinto beans

1 8- or 10-ounce can butter or
fava beans
1 4- or 6-ounce can kidney
beans
1 20- or 22-ounce can peeled
plum tomatoes with liquid
½ teaspoon salt
1 bay leaf
¼ teaspoon cracked black
pepper

In a heavy soup kettle, sauté the sausage until browned. Add the onion, carrots, and celery. Sauté, stirring occasionally, until the onion is limp, about 5 minutes. Add the remaining ingredients, reduce the heat, and simmer for 15 to 20 minutes.

Yield: 4 to 6 servings

Basque Potato Soup

Potatoes really do soothe, despite Dan Quayle's experience with the little tubers.

½ pound Italian sausage links, sliced
½ cup chopped onion
1 8-ounce can tomatoes
3 cups peeled and sliced russet potatoes (about 2 large spuds)
3 cups peeled and sliced red new potatoes
1½ cups sliced celery with tops
¼ cup chopped fresh parsley

1 clove
3 tablespoons concentrated beef stock base or 3 beef bouillon cubes diluted in 1 quart water
1 tablespoon lemon juice
1 bay leaf
¼ teaspoon sage
½ teaspoon sweet basil
1 teaspoon salt
½ teaspoon fresh ground pepper

In a large saucepan, brown the sausage over medium heat for 3 to 4 minutes. Add the onion and cook 5 minutes more. Add the remaining ingredients. Bring to a boil, reduce the heat, and simmer, uncovered, for 30 to 40 minutes, or until tender.

Yield: 4 servings

Quick Artichoke Soup

Sometimes, the Twin is just itching to use the kickstart feature on her blender. This recipe satisfies.

1 12-ounce can chicken broth
½ cup half-and-half
1 14-ounce can cream of
   chicken soup
1 8-ounce can water-packed
   artichoke hearts, drained

1 cup grated Romano cheese
¼ teaspoon salt
¼ teaspoon red pepper flakes

Combine all the ingredients in a blender and process for 45 seconds to 1 minute. Pour into a saucepan and heat over medium heat, stirring constantly. Serve hot.

Yield: 4 servings

Irish Lamb Stew

A cherished recipe of the Twin's favorite Irishwoman, Rosie O'Glutton.

2 tablespoons butter
2 pounds boneless lamb, cut into 1-inch cubes and rolled in flour
1 quart cold water
1 cup pearl onions
1 pound fresh tomatoes, peeled, seeded, and sliced
¼ cup chopped fresh parsley
3 cups peeled and diced new potatoes

2 carrots, sliced
1 white turnip, peeled and sliced
Pinch salt
1 bay leaf
Pinch fresh ground black pepper
1 cup diced fresh green beans

Melt the butter in a Dutch oven or heavy soup pan and brown the lamb cubes over medium heat. Remove the lamb and add the water to the Dutch oven, scraping the pot to deglaze. Add the remaining ingredients, except the green beans, and bring to a boil very slowly. Simmer, uncovered, for 2 hours. Add the green beans and simmer for another 7 minutes.

Yield: 4 servings

Chapter Five

✂

Erica Kane's Hair

The other day this woman who writes for soap operas was interviewed on television. The interviewer asked her why she thought so many millions of women—and men—are hooked on soaps. "Well, in so many ways their lives are just like yours and mine," she confided with a straight face. "Their lives are woven with the same tapestry of problems. You know, family, relationships, love."

Call me dull, but in my tapestry of friends, I do not know one woman named Raven. Or Luna. Or one man named Zinc, who is a count. And no millionaire–bare chested–hunk–rebel in skintight leather pants has ever sneaked into my back yard and taken me in my gazebo while I was reading Emily Dickinson.

And most important, this woman overlooked real problems: money, illness (not just amnesia, but flu, cancer, heart attacks), losing jobs, headbanger kids, and having your Evil Twin do your hair.

Erica Kane, for example, has never had a bad hair day. Never has her perm broken off as she shut the door of her limo. And if it had, she wouldn't eat; she would have the hairdresser made into luggage.

Erica Kane's Evil Twin is anorexic. She does not binge. You give her a trauma (and she's had a few—nine or ten divorces, losing her kid in a custody battle, terrorist attacks, plane crashes, a failed plan to bust her lover from prison and a heretofore unknown daughter), and food does not pass her lips.

ERICA: (Post crash, large but attractive head wound, perfect hair, strategically torn silk blouse, stiletto heels intact): "Whe . . . whe . . . where am I? Am, am, I alive—oh my God, Jack, Adam, Nick, Tom, Jeremy, Dimitri, Charlie . . . are you there, darling, *darling.*"

PILOT CAÑON: (Cruelly handsome, torn Polo sweater, burned chinos, charred croc moccs, sexy scar near left eye): "It's me, Cañon Gozinya, Ms. Kane. You're going to be all right, Ms. Kane. Here, try to eat this broth, croissant, and crème brûlée I've prepared. You need your strength."

ERICA: "No, no, I can't eat. I'm too worried about my hair. Is it just terrible?"

Here's where soaps lose credibility. For real women, a bad hair day is a prelude to tunneling through a loaf of banana bread; surely a plane crash should set Erica up for devouring a hub cap full of rocky road.

Another soap credibility gap is that heroines crave misery instead of food. To me, there is no choice between having my mother's husband's baby with a rottweiler midwife in the bulkhead of a Piper Cub airplane during a thunder-and-lightning storm, and curling up with a good book and a bag of nachos. And I could even make a case for the latter being a bigger thrill. The flaw in soaps is not that people spring back from accidents where they are decapitated, it's that they don't eat.

Once in a while, a soap heroine eats like a pack of linebackers and loses bone structure. Soon afterward she goes down in a small plane over Venezuela.

You can tell the length of a new star's contract by two things—her hairstyle and her body. If she is wearing a bob or short pageboy, and has more than a teaspooon of body fat, it is a maximum of two years, no renewal options. She will play the brief and tragic role of a good-hearted victim-type who will turn Stone's head while his bitchy skinny wife sleeps with his corporate rival at his hunting lodge that has been boarded up since 1963 but now has cupboards miraculously stocked with caviar, Brie, fresh strawberries, oysters, butter, focaccia, and champagne that they will never eat because they are too busy having sex on a Ralph Lauren blanket in front of a roaring fire.

The sweet, bobbed, bodyfatted one will listen to him, understand him, cry with him, and yes, even sleep with him, but soon she will take a job as a candy striper in a Romanian hospital. If she is carrying his child, she will die in an arson fire intended for him.

I suggest a whole new genre among afternoon TV starting with "As the Fridge Empties," where misery is salved ceremoniously with piles of breads and quickbreads and soap stars, like the rest of us, eat their way out of the long, lonely, dark, and hungry tunnel of love.

Fool for Love Hazelnut Scones

If you have never been a fool for love, the Twin does not want to break bread with you.

2⅓ cups cake flour
½ cup sugar
2 teaspoons baking powder
½ teaspoon salt
¼ teaspoon cream of tartar

6 tablespoons shortening
1 cup currants or raisins
1 cup chopped hazelnuts
2 eggs
⅓ cup heavy cream

Preheat the oven to 425° F.

Mix the flour, sugar, baking powder, salt, and cream of tartar with a wire whisk. Cut in the shortening with a pastry blender or two knives until the mixture is coarse. Stir in the currants or raisins and nuts. Separate 1 egg and reserve 1 tablespoon of the egg white. Beat the eggs, add to the flour mix with the cream and gently blend. Pat the dough to a ½- to ¾-inch thickness on a floured board. Cut into triangles or rounds and place on a greased cookie sheet. Brush the tops with the reserved egg white. Bake for 12 minutes, or until golden brown.

Yield: 10 scones

Politically Incorrect Indian

Fry Bread Crepes

Serving tip: Wear a torn rawhide sheath and eat in a canoe.

3 eggs
¼ cup water
¼ cup milk
½ cup all-purpose flour
½ cup cornmeal
1 teaspoon salt

1 tablespoon firmly packed
  brown sugar
3 tablespoons butter, melted
1½ sticks butter for frying
Honey

In a medium-size bowl, beat together the eggs, water, and milk. Add the flour, cornmeal, salt, sugar, and the 3 tablespoons of butter. Mix well. Heat a crepe pan or stick-free omelette pan on low heat for about 1 minute. Turn the heat up to medium for another minute, add 3 tablespoons of butter, coat the pan, and pour the butter out. Add ⅛ cup of the fry bread batter, coating the bottom of the pan. Remove the pan from the heat for about 20 seconds, turn the crepe with a spatula, and cook the other side for about 20 seconds. Repeat for the remaining crepes, buttering the pan as needed. Serve with honey.

Yield: 10 to 12 crepes

Coffeecake

The Twin's idea of the perfect coffee klatch: Just you, the cake, and Casablanca.

2 cups all-purpose flour
1¾ cups instant raisin and
  brown sugar oatmeal
2 tablespoons baking powder
1 cup (2 sticks) butter
1 cup firmly packed brown
  sugar
1 tablespoon regular espresso
  coffee, not brewed

1 egg
1 teaspoon pure vanilla extract
¾ cup buttermilk
1 tablespoon cinnamon
3 cups fresh or frozen
  marionberries or blueberries

Preheat the oven to 350° F. Grease a 10-inch springform pan.

Mix 1½ cups of the flour, 1 cup of the oatmeal, and the baking powder. Melt ½ cup of the butter, then blend it with ½ cup of the brown sugar, the espresso, egg, vanilla, and buttermilk. Blend in the flour mixture. Pour the cake batter into the prepared pan. Make the topping from the remaining ½ cup of brown sugar, ½ cup flour, ½ cup oatmeal, ½ cup butter (cut into cubes), and the cinnamon and blend in a food processor until crumbly. Cover the top of the cake with the berries and sprinkle with the topping. Bake for 1 hour or until a knife inserted in the middle comes out clean.

Yield: 8 servings

Therapy-Ending Poppy Seed Bread

Haven't you given your therapist enough money?

2 cups all-purpose flour
½ cup granulated sugar
2 tablespoons firmly packed
  brown sugar
2 teaspoons baking powder
1 teaspoon salt
3 tablespoons butter

3 tablespoons canola oil
1 egg
1 cup half-and-half
1 tablespoon lemon zest
  (grated lemon rind)
2 tablespoons poppy seeds

Preheat the oven to 350° F.

Sift the flour, sugars, baking powder, and salt into a bowl. In a small saucepan melt the butter and mix in the oil. Beat the egg with the half-and-half and add the melted butter and oil mixture. Stir the liquid ingredients into the dry ones until well blended. Fold in the lemon zest and poppy seeds. Bake in a greased 9 × 5-inch bread pan for 40 minutes.

Yield: 1 sweet little loaf

Street Legal Macadamia Muffins

Speaking of Hawaii, why did Annette Funicello never, ever surf?

2 cups cake flour
½ cup granulated sugar
¼ cup firmly packed brown
  sugar
¼ cup shredded coconut
1 cup chopped macadamia
  nuts

½ teaspoon baking powder
1½ sticks butter, softened
2 eggs, lightly beaten
¼ cup milk
Butter

Preheat the oven to 400° F. Line muffin cups with paper liners.

Mix together the flour, sugars, coconut, ¾ cup of the nuts, and baking powder in a large bowl. Cut in the butter until the batter has a coarse texture. Add the eggs and milk and stir until just blended. Spoon the batter into the muffin cups. Sprinkle each muffin with the remaining nuts. Bake for 10 minutes, reduce the heat to 350° F., and bake for 15 to 20 minutes, or until the tops are golden. Cool and eat with butter.

Yield: 9 to 12 muffins. Make the big ones.

Lose the Tape Measure

Cream Biscuits

And while you're at it, lose the scales, the butter substitute, the three-way mirror, the exercise video from hell . . .

2 cups biscuit baking mix
1 teaspoon baking powder
Pinch salt
¼ teaspoon nutmeg
1 tablespoon cinnamon

1 cup heavy cream, whipped
¼ cup butter, melted
1 teaspoon cinnamon mixed
with ¼ cup sugar

Mix together the biscuit mix, baking powder, salt, nutmeg, and cinnamon, then fold into the whipped cream gradually. Pat the batter out softly on a floured board to a ½-inch thickness, and cut into rounds with a biscuit cutter. Bake on a greased cookie sheet for 10 minutes, or until lightly browned. When cool enough to handle, dip the biscuit tops in melted butter and dunk in the cinnamon-sugar mixture.

Yield: 6 to 8 biscuits

Nana's Cure-all Banana Loaf

Do you know any really neurotic monkeys? Of course not.

1¾ cups all-purpose flour
2¼ teaspoons baking powder
½ teaspoon salt
⅔ cup sugar
⅓ cup butter
¼ teaspoon pure vanilla extract
¼ cup honey
1 teaspoon orange zest (grated
  orange rind)

2 eggs
2 to 3 large, overripe bananas,
  mashed
¾ cup chopped black walnuts
¼ cup chopped dates
  (optional)

Preheat the oven to 350° F.

Sift together into a bowl the flour, baking powder, and salt. In another bowl cream the sugar, butter, vanilla, and honey and add the orange zest. Beat in the eggs and bananas. Gradually add the sifted ingredients to the banana mixture. Fold in the nuts and dates. Pour the batter into a greased 9 × 5-inch bread pan and bake for 1 hour, or until a knife inserted in the center comes out clean. Cool and eat.

Yield: 1 loaf

Gestalt Zuke Bread

This hearty bread, a bowl of soup, milk, and a cheap novel is a great supper.

3 cups thinly sliced zucchini, drained on paper towels
½ cup chopped green onions
1 clove garlic, minced
1 tablespoon minced fresh tarragon
2 tablespoons minced fresh parsley
¼ cup (½ stick) butter
1 8½-ounce box corn muffin mix
½ cup grated sharp Cheddar cheese
½ cup grated sharp Monterey Jack cheese
¼ cup corn oil
3 eggs, lightly beaten
¼ cup buttermilk
½ teaspoon salt
¼ teaspoon fresh ground pepper
Optional topping: 2 ½-ounce bags (or more) Fritos Corn Chips "powdered" in the blender

Preheat the oven to 350° F.

Sauté the zucchini, onion, garlic, and herbs in the butter. Drain the liquid and let cool. Mix the zucchini mixture and the remaining ingredients together in a large bowl and pour into a greased 13 × 9 × 2-inch baking pan. Add the corn-chip topping, if desired, and bake for 30 to 35 minutes, or until golden brown. Cool, cut into squares, and eat.

Yield: 1 pan, 2 friends

Hansel and Gretel's

Revenge Gingerbread

True comfort food, gingerbread served warm with ice cream, can reverse the aging process and take you back to natal bliss.

½ cup (1 stick) butter
2 tablespoons firmly packed
  brown sugar
½ cup granulated sugar
1 egg
½ cup molasses
½ cup buttermilk
¼ cup vanilla yogurt

1⅔ cups cake flour
¾ teaspoon baking soda
¼ teaspoon salt
½ teaspoon cinnamon
1½ teaspoons ginger
½ teaspoon allspice
Vanilla ice cream

Preheat the oven to 350° F.

Cream the butter and sugars. Add the egg and beat until smooth and creamy. Add the molasses and beat until well blended. Mix the buttermilk with the yogurt. Sift together the dry ingredients and add them to the egg mixture alternately with the buttermilk mixture.

Line the bottom of an 8 × 8 × 2-inch baking pan with wax paper; grease the paper and the sides of the pan lightly. Pour the batter into the pan and bake for 25 to 30 minutes, or until a knife inserted in the center comes out clean. Serve warm with vanilla ice cream.

Yield: 8 servings

☎

Chapter Six

Dumped but Never Stumped: The Twin's Dos and Don'ts

Most of the time your Evil Twin should have her way with you. Petulant little hussy, she will act out anyway, run her course, and retreat until Mercury has a bellyful of retrograde. Her actions, however despicable, may be what are keeping you from a padded room. Attempts to suppress her are like tampering with a bad perm; any shot at improvement will further mutate the outcome. But listen, because this is important. There is one time when you need to harness your Twin's cries for attention and sit on her hard. When you've been dumped.

When you've been dumped you aren't in your right mind, and

neither is your Twin. Both of you are working without a net and you could wind up doing things that 1) get you thrown into the slammer; 2) get you thrown into a straitjacket; or 3) force you to join the Witness Protection Program.

Some of us lick our wounds by retreating with fudge cake and old Righteous Brothers albums. This is okay—for a while. Others take a walk on the wild side. This is bad if it lasts more than a couple of weeks. Calling his house and hanging up, ordering a dossier on the new woman, and stalking his every move will erode your self-esteem and wear down a good pair of pumps. Inching onto the ledge of his high-rise apartment Garbo-style only works if you are attached to a bungee cord.

My friend PK especially advises against indiscriminate sex in order to prove you're womanly and desirable. "Every man I'd ever known was fair game—the mailman, the meter reader, the lawn boy. Old friends would drop by for coffee and I'd drag them off to bed. I ruined some of my oldest and best friendships," she laments, her face smeared with a cream puff.

Try to remember that getting dumped happens to everybody. You will get over it, and chances are, you'll find someone much better for you. But in the meantime, ask your closest friends to pitch a stakeout outside your place and when they see you slip out at three a.m. in a black catsuit and suction cups on your shoes, shoot to kill.

Meanwhile, these few simple guidelines should alert you to the Evil Twin's skewed idea of recovery.

WHAT THE TWIN WANTS YOU TO DO

WHY YOU SHOULD NOT

Get a Glenn Close–style *Fatal Attraction* hairdo

Suggests a frenzied, feral attitude that says "I was just dumped and you will have to spend every night listening to my unrelenting tears and the story of how I gave him all of me which is something I rarely do and he hurt me anyway, and you won't, *will you? Will you? Will you?*"

Date boys

You will have to drive.

Join an expensive health spa and wear a ridiculous workout leotard thong that looks like butt floss

The club will be filled with people who think life's problems can be solved by increasing muscle to fat ratio, and the thong will bug you.

Stalk his house/studio/apartment even if it's in a high-rise on the eighteenth floor

You could be road hash or you could be arrested. You are not a desperate woman.

Call him at three a.m. to tell him you're glad you can still be friends.	It's a big-time lie.
Burn *her* initials in his yard while wearing a pointed white hat and cape	Remember how short capes make you look.
Grovel	Save it for speeding tickets.
Do something permanent to the new girlfriend	You look bad in prison gray.
Liposuction	Shouldn't he be the one practicing self-mutilation?

It's true, being dumped hurts. Everywhere you turn people come in twos. The world suddenly looks like a Noah's Ark audition. Lovers, two by two, grinding espresso together at the market, walking large rambunctious dogs, locking eyes over the pinot noir. You have a feeling of belonging to no one, with no prospects for better days. Things will get better. They always do. Instead of wasting all that energy on someone who wasn't good enough for you anyway, let your Twin out and blow through a few healthy denial-based fantasies together.

May I suggest the supermarket . . .

CHECK-OUT BOY: Well, ma'am, will that be all today?

TWIN: Zat, and you leek me from ze toes up. Zen zat weel be all today, my leetle pleasure noodle.

REALITY: Why, yes, thank you. Have a good day.

Or the office . . .

YOUR BOSS: Are you having a problem with time management?

TWIN: Only to ze degree zat you're having a pwoblem wiz nostril hairs.

REALITY: Not at all. I have everything under control now, and I think you'll be pleased with the results of this project.

While you're waiting for denial to run its course, assess all your great points like expressive hands, a sense of humor, and being a good friend. Then, to grease the route to re-entry, you and the Twin need to hunker down with something you deserve, something soothing, warm, and savory.

The Golden Door Spa's Secret

Fat-Busting Chickie

Okay, so it's not from a spa. Give yourself a facial after you eat it.

1 6- to 8-pound stewing chicken, cut in pieces
1 bay leaf
¼ cup butter, melted
¼ cup all-purpose flour
1½ teaspoons salt
½ teaspoon cracked black pepper

1 clove garlic, crushed
2 cups chicken stock
1 8-ounce package flat, wide egg noodles, cooked
1 cup soft buttered bread crumbs
1 cup grated Cheddar cheese

Simmer the chicken in enough water to cover by 2 inches with the bay leaf, covered, until the meat drops from the bones, about 2 hours. When cool enough, remove the skin and bones and discard. Cut the meat into large pieces. In a bowl, blend the butter, flour, salt, pepper, and garlic. Gradually stir in the chicken stock.

Drain the noodles and arrange in a baking dish in alternating layers with the chicken. Pour the sauce over all. Preheat the oven to 350° F.

Spread the bread crumbs and cheese over the top and bake for 10 to 15 minutes, or until nicely browned.

Yield: 6 servings

A (Crash) Course in

Miracles Onion Pie

Two bites. Truth happens.

1 sleeve saltine crackers
1½ cups (1½ sticks) butter, melted
2 cups chopped yellow onions
6 slices pepper bacon (see Note) or regular bacon diced and cooked

2 eggs, well beaten
½ cup sour cream
½ cup half-and-half
1 tablespoon all-purpose flour
1 teaspoon sugar
½ teaspoon salt
¼ teaspoon paprika

Preheat the oven to 375° F.

Make a crust by placing the saltines in a blender and whipping until "powdered." Place in a greased 8 inch pie pan and pour 1 cup of the melted butter evenly around the bottom and sides. Press mixture onto the bottom and sides of the pan to make a pie shell.

Sauté the onions in the remaining ½ cup of melted butter until just soft but not brown. Add the pepper bacon to the onions and set aside to cool. Beat the eggs, sour cream, half-and-half, flour, sugar, salt, and paprika together. Spread the onion mixture over the crust, pour on the egg mixture, and bake for 15 minutes.

Reduce the heat to 350° F. and bake for another 15 minutes, or until the pie is nicely browned. Serve hot.

Yield: 6 servings

Note: Pepper bacon can be found in the deli or butcher section of the market.

Devilish Angel Hair Pasta Pie

This is so easy and so impressive. A chewy, cheesy, and cheap main dish.

9-ounce package angel hair
    pasta, cooked al dente (see
    Note) and drained
3 tablespoons butter, melted
¼ cup half-and-half

½ cup grated Parmesan cheese
½ cup grated Romano cheese
¼ teaspoon nutmeg
Squeeze of lemon
Salt and pepper

Preheat the oven to 400° F.

    Toss all the ingredients together in a large bowl and press into a generously buttered glass 9-inch pie plate. Bake for 45 minutes.

    Remove from the oven and let sit 7 to 10 minutes.

Yield: 6 servings

Note: Just done, or done "to the tooth."

Camp Crybaby Hamburger Nests

Remember when Karen Sullivan told on you for wetting your pants at camp? May she never savor one of these nests.

Catsup
½ pound lean ground beef
1 carrot, chopped
1 small yellow onion, chopped
1 medium potato, peeled and
  chopped
1 tablespoon Worcestershire
  sauce

Salt and coarsely ground black
  pepper
1 chunk Cheddar or smoked
  Gouda cheese

Preheat the oven to 400° F.

Pour a blob of catsup on a 10 × 10-inch piece of heavy-duty aluminum foil. Shape the ground meat into a patty and put it on the catsup. Add the vegetables, Worcestershire sauce, salt, and pepper and top with the cheese. Bake for 45 minutes to an hour. Let cool a few minutes before eating. Pour on more catsup.

Yield: 1 nest

Creamy Beef Stroganoff

Yes, it's fattening. Yes, it's dated. Yes, Hazel made it for Mister B. Give it a new twist. Cook it while wearing a majorette uniform.

1 pound lean beef, cut in ¼-inch strips
Olive oil for frying
1 cup sliced large mushrooms
½ cup sliced carrots
1 cup sliced-in-strips bell pepper
1 12-ounce bottle dark ale
¼ cup sour cream
½ teaspoon basil
¼ teaspoon fennel seeds
1 teaspoon Kitchen Bouquet
1 tablespoon burnt sugar (see Note)
2 cups cooked egg noodles

In a skillet, brown the beef in the olive oil. Add the mushrooms, carrots, and peppers and sauté for about 2 minutes. Blend in all the remaining ingredients except the noodles, cover, and simmer for 5 to 7 minutes. Serve over the cooked noodles.

Yield: 4 servings

Note: Burn the sugar by holding it in a soup spoon or ladle over a stove burner on high for just a few seconds. Use an oven mitt. When the sugar starts to sizzle and burn, add it to the Stroganoff.

Maharishi Blake's Meat Loaf

Blake is a modern, centered, self-actualized woman who works off this meat loaf by tap dancing to Elvis Presley's "Hunka, Hunka Burnin' Love."

1 pound lean ground beef
1 12-ounce package pork
  sausage with sage
½ cup unsweetened
  applesauce
½ cup mashed potato flakes
1 cup chopped onion
1 cup chopped bell pepper,
  any color

1 egg
½ cup corn flakes
4 ounces sharp Cheddar
  cheese, cubed
¼ cup catsup
Pinch salt and pepper

Preheat the oven to 325° F.

In a large bowl, mix all the ingredients together until well blended. Put into two 8 × 4-inch loaf pans and bake for about 1 hour, or until well browned. About 5 minutes before you remove the loaf, spread a little additional catsup over the top.

Yield: 2 loaves. Freeze 1 for wonderful sandwiches.

Angst-Buster Risotto

This dish has a dramatic, mysterious, Fellini-movie quality, even though no one in his movies ever eats.

1 cup raw Arborio rice
2 tablespoons butter
3 to 4 cups rich, good-quality
  chicken broth, heated
Salt and pepper to taste

¼ cup cubed Havarti cheese
½ cup grated Asagio cheese
1 tablespoon lemon juice
¼ cup toasted almonds

In a large saucepan, cook the rice in the butter over medium heat for 1 minute, stirring constantly. Add the broth, cover, and simmer over low heat until tender, 25 to 30 minutes. The rice should be creamy on the outside but al dente on the inside. (Translated: soft enough to lodge in your dental work.) Put the rice in a bowl, add a dash of salt and pepper, and toss with the cheeses, lemon juice, and almonds. Serve warm.

Yield: 4 servings

C. Everett Koop's Private

Reserve Mac and Cheese

Unmold and fill the center of this clever dish with any food that goes well with cheese. Examples: Creamed peas, mushrooms, chopped ham, biscotti, hamburgers, milkshakes, martinis . . .

1 cup dry bread crumbs
½ cup hot half-and-half
½ cup Miracle Whip salad
   dressing or mayonnaise
1 tablespoon butter, melted
1 cup macaroni, ziti, or penne,
   cooked and drained
1 cup grated Cheddar cheese
¼ cup grated Monterey Jack
   cheese

¼ cup grated Parmesan cheese
½ cup chopped black olives
1 onion, chopped
2 tablespoons chopped fresh
   parsley
2 eggs, well beaten
Dash Tabasco
Salt and pepper

Preheat the oven to 350° F.

Soak the crumbs in the half-and-half, Miracle Whip, and butter. Add to the hot macaroni along with the remaining ingredients and toss well. Pour into a greased 1-quart ring mold and set the pan in a larger pan of warm water. Bake for 40 minutes, or until firm.

Yield: 4 to 6 servings

Basque Pizza

There is something about the musty, fragrant taste of these ingredients that makes you want to run away with a poet/shepherd.

1 pound cooked Italian
sausage
2 baked sweet potatoes,
peeled and cubed
½ cup heavy cream
2 teaspoons sugar
3 cloves garlic, minced
½ teaspoon oregano leaves
½ teaspoon basil
1 teaspoon tarragon

3 tablespoons chopped fresh
parsley
½ cup grated Parmesan cheese
½ cup grated smoked Gouda
1 small sweet red onion, sliced
thin
2 tablespoons olive oil
1 large, round sourdough
bread

Preheat the oven to 375° F.

In a large bowl, mix all the ingredients together, except the bread. Cut the top off of the bread and scoop out a cavity. Fill the cavity with the sausage mixture, place the "lid" back on, and bake on a cookie sheet for 15 to 20 minutes. Cool slightly and slice in wedges.

Yield: 8 servings

99

The Dalai Lama's

Kosher Corned Beef

According to legend, the next Dalai Lama must recite the ingredients in this recipe to prove he is the chosen one.

1 3½- to 4-pound brisket of corned beef
1 12-ounce bottle Guinness Stout ale

1 tablespoon balsamic vinegar
15 to 20 dried green peppercorns

Marinate the brisket overnight in the Guinness Stout.

Place the brisket and Guinness in a Dutch oven, add the balsamic vinegar and peppercorns, and bring to a boil over medium heat. Simmer, covered, for about 3½ hours, or 1 hour per pound of beef.

Yield: 8 servings

Chapter Seven

The Evil Twin as Personal Shopper

You may have noticed there are days when your Evil Twin is missing. No hair bumps. Single portions satisfy. You buy a geranium for the blond French aerobics teacher, Yvette, who just leased the apartment next door. You can stare down a plate of cinnamon rolls.

On these days, your Evil Twin is busy as your personal shopper. She is cruising department stores with your man, searching for the perfect gift. The one that makes you look like a parolee who just got layaway privileges.

Okay, you're thinking, I'm lucky to have a man who buys me

anything. Don't be so critical. So what if an occasional gift is a little off? It's sweet. Cute, even.

It's precisely this "off" that throws us. Here is a typical pattern of gifts:

Birthday: 6,000 hp Black & Decker Tree Shredder
Promotion: Pearl earrings
Christmas: Satin nightie
Anniversary: A dozen red roses
Valentine's Day: Black shelf bra with stereophonic nipples
Mother's Day: Blender

One night at my house, we model our gifts. Lynn, who wears only the clothes by Italian designers, still irons her sheets, and runs ten miles in large cultured pearl studs, got a mustard-yellow fanny pack that says "Lookin' Hot" across it in neon green letters. Not terrible, just a bit surreal, like seeing Audrey Hepburn in dreadlocks. She explains it as a natural consequence of the Date Lie. Date Lies are told when you are just beginning to go out with a man who is nuts about the outdoors and you are convincing him that if only you could climb Everest, you could die whole.

Belle is wearing a snappy little fräulein number, a flowered cotton dress stretched tight and low across her big bosom, and closed with string like an old (too-tight) sneaker. She is an accountant and CEO of her own company, but tonight she looks like the star of porn videos that you might find under the beds of pubescent German boys. PK has on a shelf bra, the likes of which we've not seen since Betty on "Father Knows Best." Sam is revving up her shop-vac. Blake, who is five feet one, is sitting on the floor wearing a green velveteen cape. The end of the cape is closed in the door of her car. "He must think I'm taller," she explains.

Size is often the Evil Twin's chief tweak.

To the modern saleswoman, the confused-looking man who strolls into her department unchaperoned represents her entire Christmas Club account in one pop. The clerks know the look. He wanders aimlessly around the women's department at dusk on Christmas Eve. It is time to buy the *gift*.

Limbic brain fully engaged, his eyes are glazed over, his hands fondle anything with a bright color or a sexy texture. The Twin, meanwhile, is eyeing the inventory from 1982.

"I'm looking for a gift for my wife," he says.

"What size is she?" asks the clerk.

The Twin is salivating.

His answer, whether the saleswoman is a former Amazon warrior or is standing on the display case to talk to him, never varies. "She's about your size."

Instantly, the world's women become one size fits all. "Yeah, your size," he says gazing at her sky-blue blouse, "and her favorite color is blue." This woman is smart. This woman is trained to move inventory. This woman has a perfect abstract cubist haircut which costs $1,000 a month to maintain. This woman will meet her quota.

Which is why, as I write this, I am sitting in my size 2 pair of electric blue velveteen jodhpurs that come with a yeast infection disclaimer. There is nothing left for me to do but pour cake mix on my tongue and bury my head in a bag of nachos. I need a last resort.

White Trash Pots de Crème

This combination satisfies that odd recurring anguish—things like your obsession with where your first bicycle went or wondering if you had a chive on your tooth at your poetry reading.

8 paper muffin cups
2 Devil's Food Roll Cake
  Cookies or Hostess cupcakes

2 Dove Bar Rondos or ice
  cream bon bons

Put 3 or 4 paper muffin cups inside one another to make a sturdier cup. Make 2 sets. Place 1 cookie or cupcake in each cup and microwave on medium-low heat for 30 seconds. Add a Dove Bar Rondo to each, pushing it down into the cake. Microwave on medium heat for another 10 seconds. Stir gently and eat.

Yield: 2 pots de crème

Reggie's Just Say No

Swedish Crème

2 cups plus 6 tablespoons
  heavy cream
1 cup sugar
1 teaspoon unflavored gelatin
1 pint sour cream

1 teaspoon pure vanilla extract
2 cups fresh blueberries,
  marionberries, or
  strawberries

In a medium saucepan, mix the cream, sugar, and gelatin and heat for 5 minutes over low heat. Remove and cool until the mixture thickens to a pudding consistency. Fold in the sour cream and gently stir in the vanilla. In each of four goblets, place ½ cup of the fruit. Pour the crème mixture over and chill for at least 10 minutes before eating.

Yield: 4 servings

Chocolate-Coated Nutty Nanas

This conjures up images of state fairs with their cheap but fragrant food and two-headed babies in jars of formaldehyde.

1 8-ounce jar chocolate ice
  cream topping

1 banana
¼ cup crushed walnuts

Follow microwave directions for melting chocolate topping in the jar. Peel the banana three-quarters of the way down and stick the banana in the chocolate. Roll in nuts. Eat.

Yield: 1 serving

Peanut Butter Macaroni Salad

A favorite of Cleopatra's, this salad was credited with giving her her youthful skin and sweet breath.

2 cups hot cooked macaroni
¼ cup soft peanut butter
¼ cup soy sauce
3 tablespoons Miracle Whip
  salad dressing

1 tablespoon sesame seeds
Salt and pepper to taste
Dash red pepper flakes
  (optional)

Mix all the ingredients together and eat while warm.

Yield: 2 servings

Birdseed

Note: This bag is not a toy. *Do not keep your head immersed in it after you've eaten the contents. And while you're at it, don't tear the tags off your mattresses and pillows, either.*

1 8-ounce can beer nuts
1 cup semisweet chocolate
  chips

Mix the nuts and chocolate chips together in a plastic bag and shake.

Yield: 1 to 2 servings

Graham Crackers with Icing

Seems to do the trick after being caught in freezing rain or discovering that all the shoes you just paid $200 a pair for look completely violent.

6 graham crackers, split
3 tablespoons vanilla icing or
  cream cheese

¼ cup cold semisweet
  chocolate chips

Spread the icing or cream cheese on half of the graham cracker pieces, shake on the chips, and cover with the remaining pieces.

Yield: 1 serving of 3 sandwiches

The Queen's Petit Fours

The combination of sweet and salty may just anesthetize you after the perm from hell.

12 Ritz crackers
Peanut butter, smooth or
  crunchy

6 to 8 ounces white candy
  coating (see Note)

Spread the crackers with the peanut butter and press together to make 6 "sandwiches."

In a heavy saucepan, melt the candy over medium to low heat. Using tongs, dip the sandwiches in the melted candy, remove, and cool on their sides on wax paper. Refrigerate for at least 5 minutes.

Yield: 2 servings

Note: Some stores carry this only at Christmas. If so, bullwhip your grocer.

Cellulite-Busting Pralines

Creamy, sweet, and nutty, these are a craving to plan ahead for. Then, when your rent goes up, you'll be ready.

2 tablespoons butter
2 cups sugar
1 cup maple syrup
⅔ cup half-and-half
¼ teaspoon salt

½ teaspoon pure vanilla extract
1 cup chopped pecans
1 cup chopped macadamia
  nuts

Melt the butter in the top of a large double boiler over low heat. Add the sugar, syrup, and half-and-half. Stir until the sugar is dissolved. Bring to a boil and, without stirring, boil to a soft ball stage (238° F.). Remove from the heat and let stand until cool. Add the salt and vanilla. Stir with a wooden spoon until the candy begins to harden, then place over hot water and stir until soft. Add the nuts. Drop from a spoon in 3-inch rounds onto a buttered baking sheet. Chill.

Yield: 15 to 18 pralines

Note: To determine the soft ball stage, drop a little of the candy mixture into ice water. It should form a ball that doesn't dissolve, and flattens between your fingers when removed.

Luv Slave Toffee

Chewy and sweet, and jaw-punishing, this toffee is a private sacrament.

2 cups firmly packed brown
  sugar
1 cup dark Karo syrup
½ cup (1 stick) butter

2 tablespoons sweetened
  condensed milk
1 8-ounce chocolate bar
(optional)

Cook all the ingredients except the chocolate bar over low heat until the soft crack stage (290° F.). Remove and pour into a greased 9-inch pie pan and refrigerate. If desired, melt the chocolate bar and pour over the top.

Yield: Serves 4

Note: At the soft crack stage, the mixture dropped into ice water will separate into hard threads that bend when removed.

Tawdry Tortillas

This satisfies that craving for salty, spicy, and crunchy tastes, and also works as a fine floor wax.

1 green onion, chopped
1 green chile, chopped
2 tablespoons grated cheese of your choice
1 avocado, sliced
4 smashed nacho chips

¼ cup toasted pumpkin seeds (optional)
1 tablespoon mayonnaise or Miracle Whip salad dressing
1 soft flour tortilla
½ cup salsa

Place the onion, chile, cheese, avocado, chips, seeds, if using, and mayo on the tortilla and fold. Microwave for 1 minute on high. Dip in salsa.

Yield: 1 tortilla

Blake's Pickle

Okay, so it's not for everybody. Neither is Armand Assante.

1 dill pickle
1 jar soft peanut butter

Dip. Eat.

Yield: 1 serving

Butter-Fried Tater Sticks

The Twin suggests serving at divorce showers.

1 2.8-ounce can potato sticks
1 2.8-ounce can onion rings
2 tablespoons butter

Salt and pepper
½ cup grated cheese of choice
Catsup

Fry the potato sticks and onion rings in butter over medium heat. Add salt, pepper, and cheese. Toss and eat with catsup.

Yield: 1 serving

Robert Bly's Wildwoman

Nut Crunches

One bite and you have a strong urge to play the drums—bongos.

1 egg
1 cup sugar
1 cup chopped pecans

2 1.4-ounce Heath candy bars,
   smashed into pieces
5 tablespoons all-purpose flour

Preheat the oven to 375° F.

Beat the egg and sugar in bowl. Add the nuts, Heath bar, and flour and stir. Drop the mixture by teaspoonfuls onto a lightly greased nonstick cookie sheet. Bake 9 to 10 minutes. Let cool. Wonderful crumbled up on ice cream.

Yield: 10 to 12 crunches

Mainline Malted

The only liquid diet endorsed by the Twin.

1½ cups whole milk
¼ cup chocolate syrup

2 scoops vanilla ice cream
¼ cup malted milk powder

Pour the milk, syrup, 1 scoop of the ice cream, and the malted milk powder into the blender and process on high for 5 seconds. Add the second scoop of ice cream and blend for another 5 seconds.

Yield: 1 large or 2 small malteds

❀

Making Peace with Your Twin, or How to Have Fewer Personalities Than Sybil

Wow! Who was that masked woman, you ask, still drunk with the orgasmic high of chocolate eclairs. One minute you were in balance, paying off your charge cards and feeding the rest of the cherry pie to the dog. The next, you were melting cake mix on your tongue. Well, that's the rub with the Twin; she wins. The sooner you accept this, the sooner she lightens up. So let's make peace with her and get on with more important things like feeding kids and making power dressing a dim memory.

But don't confuse making peace with your Twin with nurturing your inner child. Repeating silly affirmations, sleeping with a teddy bear, and giving yourself permission to skip will get you, at best, charging privileges at Laura Ashley.

The Twin ate your inner child years ago and thinks it's hilarious that you are still trying to find her.

No, to salve the Twin, don't waste your time on therapy, trance channelers, past-life regressors, or liquid diets. Join her. Give her some space. Integrate, as Jung offered, your shadow self.

The possibilities are endless.

The Twin can conjure up more trouble than Barbie ever thought could exist when she was back there in that convertible and tiara, nibbling on carrots.

But just like the imaginary playmate you loved as a kid, the Twin can also be an ally. She will help you sit on your personality at somber occasions, or conversely, order you to scarf down a pan of brownies when the blind date takes you to a tractor pull—if you treat her right. That means feeding her the four basic food groups: fat, chocolate, sugar, and ibuprofen. If your cupboards are full and your humor high, you and your Twin will enjoy a long and happy relationship.

When you reach your twilight years, the Twin's antics turn to performing bogus marriage ceremonies for sweet young couples, shoplifting chopped liver for your cat, and bouts of dressing like Madonna under your pink dotted Swiss housecoat. You will appease her with creamy custards and strawberry tarts, and she will lay low while you babysit the grandkids.

You will enter the blithe currents of life, finally at peace with yourself and your thighs. You will not care how many custards you eat, or that you've had three sundaes in one day. This is when your Twin finally departs, when she will lay in wait for the next Barbie-loving pubescent kid, who does not yet realize that 38–21–36 is more likely a lottery pick than a female form, that chocolate is a gateway drug, and that life is filled with flavor.

Index

Index

Index

Index

Index

Index